Facebook

C000131931

Portal Mini

User Manual

The Complete Illustrated, Practical Guide with
Tips & Tricks to Maximizing your Portal Mini

Gilbert J. Kearns

Contents

Introduction

Facebook Portal Mini is a communication device with the key objective of making it easier for users to connect with friends and family. Three of the devices are display units comparable to the Amazon Echo Show.

Designed to resemble digital photo frames, these devices work as elegant, intelligent displays while they wait for you to make or receive a call. Though their main focus is on video calling, they also offer additional functions

First things first, let's find out how to get started with your very own Facebook Portal.

What account can I use to set up my Portal?

You need a Facebook account or a WhatsApp account to set up your Portal. Some features, including "Hey Portal," Facebook Watch, Facebook Gaming, Facebook Live and

Superframe customization aren't available when you set up your Portal with WhatsApp only or when a WhatsApp-only login exists on a shared device.

What do I need to set up my Portal?

To set up your Portal, you need the following:

- A Portal Mini

- Your Portal's power cord.

- A Facebook account or WhatsApp account.

- A high-speed, wireless internet connection.

- A clean, flat and stable location to place your Portal device.

Setting Up Your Portal

Assemble your Portal:

1. Place your Portal on a stable flat surface, like a tabletop or counter.

- Do not place your Portal near sinks, showers, pools or other areas where it might get wet.

- Do not place your Portal near sources of heat, such as stoves, ovens, or radiators.

- Do not place Portal where it may be tipped over easily.

2. Plug your Portal in with the included power cord.

- Plug the included power cord into Portal first, then into an appropriate outlet.

  - Make sure the included power cord is fully plugged into your Portal before plugging it into an appropriate outlet.

- Your Portal works when connected to a rated AC power source with 100V to 240V AC at 50Hz to 60Hz.

○ Arrange any cables and cords so that people and pets are not likely to trip over or accidentally pull on them as they move around or walk near the Portal.

Select your language and connect to Wi-Fi:

Once your Portal is plugged in, follow the on-screen instructions to begin setup.

1. Select your language, then tap **Next.**

2. Connect to Wi-Fi.

   1. Select your Wi-Fi network.

   2. Enter your Wi-Fi password and tap **Join.**

   3. Tap **Next.**

   4. Tap **Continue.** Your Portal may need to download the latest software in order to complete setup. Once the download is

complete, you may be asked to restart your Portal.

Give your Portal a name and log in with Facebook or WhatsApp:

Follow the on-screen instructions to continue setup.

1. Give your Portal a name. Tap an option from the menu or tap to create a **Custom Name,** then tap **Next.**

2. Log in with Facebook or WhatsApp:

   1. Tap the box next to Facebook or WhatsApp, then tap **Next**.

   2. Follow the on-screen instructions.

How to Control Where People Call You

Using the Home and Away function, you can ensure people only call you when you are home. With this feature on, any calls to the device will automatically be transferred to your phone when you are out. To turn it on:

- Go to "Settings"

- Select "Incoming Call Settings"

- Tap "Only When You're Home"

- An alert will pop up on your phone confirming that you want to use the Home and Away feature. Tap it to confirm

Facebook Watch

With the Facebook Portal, you get access to its YouTube competitor, Watch. It is a great way to stay abreast of recent developments as there are a lot of services out there which use Facebook.

But you will have even greater access to viral videos as well as comedy. At present, the platform does not have quite as many content creators as YouTube and there are no original series (think Hulu and Netflix).

Using Watch, you can also enjoy watching videos with your friends and family while on a call.

Games

Facebook Portal also offers some of the instant games available on Messenger. These include Sudoku, Battleship, Draw Something, and Words with Friends, among others.

How do I add or remove accounts from my Portal?

You can have up to 4 accounts linked to your Portal. The accounts you add must be Facebook friends.

Only invite people you trust to add an account to your Portal. When someone adds an account, they'll become another owner of your Portal, and they'll be able to:

- See, hear, and delete all of your Portal's voice interactions in Portal Settings or on their Facebook Activity Log.

- Make changes to voice interaction settings on your Portal, which will apply to your voice interactions.

- Use and change other settings on your Portal, which may apply across your Portal.

- Add accounts to or remove accounts from your Portal, which could include removing your account.

- Add photos or connect to third party services on your Portal.

- View and access any information you use or access on your Portal, including the ability to view and call your contacts.

Also, when someone adds an account on your Portal, their Facebook friends and Messenger connections will become contacts on your Portal, and you will be able to call their contacts.

To add an account to your Portal:

8

1. From **Home** on your Portal, tap **Settings**.

2. Tap the **Accounts** tab.

3. Tap **Add Account**.

4. Follow the on-screen instructions to confirm your Facebook account.

5. Tap **Next**.

6. Select the person you'd like to add to your Portal. If you don't see the person you'd like to add, use the **Search** option to find who you're looking for.

7. Have the person you'd like to add to your Portal tap **Log in with Facebook.**

8. Have the person you'd like to add follow the on-screen instruction to log in with their Facebook account.

To remove an account from your Portal:

1. From **Home** on your Portal, tap **Settings.**

2. Tap the **Accounts** tab.

3. Tap **Remove** next to the account you'd like to remove and follow the on-screen instructions.

Notes:

- You can also remove your own account from your Portal from the Security and Login menu in your Facebook settings. If your Facebook account is deleted, deactivated or you change your Facebook password, your account will also be removed from your Portal.

- Anyone who uses your Portal, not just another owner, can view and call all contacts, manage favorites, see photos added to your Portal, and use third-party services connected to your Portal.

- Removing an account from your Portal will remove the contacts, photos and other data associated with that account, and will remove the account holder from certain connected third party apps.

- Removing all accounts that are connected to a Portal will automatically factory reset that Portal.

- If one of multiple account holders is removed from your Portal, call history on the Portal will remain but it will no longer show that the removed account holder initiated a call.

How does calling work on Portal?

Calling Basics

With Portal, you can make and receive calls to and from your Facebook friends and WhatsApp contacts. You can't call Messenger connections that do not have Facebook accounts.

Currently, Portal calls can only be received on Portal devices, on the Messenger app on mobile phones or tablets, on messenger.com or facebook.com, or on WhatsApp on mobile phones. Calling on messenger.com or facebook.com is only available using the browsers Chrome or Opera.

Using Voice Interactions

To make a call:

Say "Hey Portal, call [contact name]." For example, "Hey Portal, call John Doe."

"Hey Portal" may ask you to confirm which contact you're trying to call by saying "Yes", "No" or by saying the full name of the contact you're trying to call.

To answer a call:

Say "Hey Portal, answer."

To end a call you can say things like:

- "Hey Portal, hang up."

- "Hey Portal, end call."

- "Hey Portal, cancel."

To make a call:

1. From **Home**, tap to open the **Contacts** app. You can filter your contacts by **Suggested**, **Recent**, **Messenger** and **WhatsApp**.

2. Tap the contact you'd like to call.

3. Tap **Video** to start your call.

To answer a call:

When receiving a call, tap **Answer** to join the call.

To end a call:

1. During a call, tap your Portal screen to expose the call menu.

2. Tap to end the call.

How do I call someone using their Facebook relationship name or nickname?

If you've added someone to the **Family and Relationships** section of your Facebook profile, you can call them on Portal using voice controls and your relationship name (or common synonyms for those names). Any relationship names on Facebook can be used.

For example, you can call your mother by saying either:

- "Hey Portal, call my mother."

- "Hey Portal, call Mom."

Notes:

- If you list a Facebook friend as your family member or that you're in a relationship with them, that person will be asked to confirm your relationship on Facebook.

- In order to use relationship names in voice commands, your relationship must be shared with your Facebook Friends or shared as Public to be associated with a contact on your Portal.

How do I create or edit a custom nickname on Portal?

When you create or edit a custom nickname, the nickname will show up wherever the contact is referenced on your Portal, like your call history and suggested contacts.

To create or edit a custom nickname:

1. From **Home** on your Portal, tap the contact you'd like to rename.

2. Tap ⠀⠀.

3. Tap ✎ **Add Nickname**.

4. Add a custom nickname using the onscreen keyboard.

5. Tap **Save**. You can now call the contact using their custom nickname.

How do I use AR Effects during a call on my Portal?

15

You can use **AR Effects** like filters and masks during a call on your Portal. If you use **AR Effects,** they will only appear on the person who added the Effect. Shared Effects appear on everyone, but are only available when everyone on the call is using Portal.

To use AR Effects or Shared Effects during a call:

1. Tap the screen to show the call menu.

2. Tap and then tap **Effects** or **Shared Effects**.

3. Tap the Effect you'd like to try.

To stop using Effects or Shared Effects during a call: Tap the screen to expose the call menu.

1. Tap **Stop** to stop using Effects or Shared Effects.

If Shared Effects don't appear during a call: Make sure everyone on the call is using Portal.

How do I turn the camera and microphone off on Portal?

To mute or unmute the camera and microphone using the touch screen during a call:

1. Tap the screen to expose the call menu.

2. Tap or to mute or unmute your camera or microphone.

To mute or unmute the camera and microphone on Portal and Portal Mini:

To turn off the camera or microphone, slide the switch on top of Portal's frame all the way to the left. A red light lets you know the camera and microphone are both off.

To turn off just the camera, slide the switch on top of Portal's frame into the middle position. You will see a shutter covering the camera's lens when you've turned the camera off.

How do I use Story Time on my Portal?

On Portal, Story Time allows you to share interactive stories with animations, music and effects during a call or using the Story Time app.

To use Story Time during a call:

1. Tap the screen to expose the call menu.

2. Tap and then tap **Story Time**.

3. Tap the story you'd like to share.

4. Tap **Play**   to   start   the   story,   or **Description** to see a brief description of the story.

To use the Story Time app:

1. From **Home**, tap the Story Time app.

2. Tap the story you'd like to start.

18

3. Tap **Play** and follow the on-screen instructions.

Notes:

- Stories can take up to 45 seconds to load.

- To use the Story Time app, enable your microphone and camera.

- If you experience trouble loading a story or see a loading signal in the middle of a story, check your internet connection.

What is Superframe on Portal?

When you're not on a call, Portal's Superframe can display photos of you and your friends and family

Superframe allows you to:

- Display photos when your Portal is idle.

- See when your closest contacts are available to connect.

- View album artwork if you're listening to music.

- See the current time and weather for your area.

- Receive birthday reminders for your friends on Facebook.

- See tips for using Portal.

How do I manage Superframe photos using the Portal app?

1. Open the app and tap your Portal.

2. Tap **Superframe.**

3. Tap ⬤ next to any albums you'd like to add to or remove from Superframe.

If you're managing Superframe photos using the Portal app:

- You can upload up to 20 photos to Superframe at once.

- You cannot add or delete photos when an upload is in progress.

- Photos you upload from the camera roll will only be displayed in the Portal app and on your household device.

To create an album in Superframe using the Portal app:

1. Open the app and tap your Portal.

2. Tap **Create Album.**

3. Tap **Add Photos,** select photos from your camera roll, then tap **Add**.

4. Tap ⬤next to **Display in Superframe.**

How can I add photos to Superframe that I don't want to share on Facebook?

You can add any of your Facebook photo albums to Superframe on Portal, including albums you've set to **Only Me**_under your photo privacy settings.

Notes:

21

- Friends tagged in **Only Me** posts will receive a Facebook notification and will be able to see the post.

- Facebook may suggest tags for photos, even when set to **Only Me**, so make sure to manually remove all tags before finalizing and posting your album if you don't want the photos seen outside your Portal.

How do I edit the privacy settings for my photos on Facebook?

Keep in mind that some photos, like your current profile photo and cover photo, are always public.

To edit the privacy settings for your photos:

1. From your News Feed, click your name in the top left to go to your profile.

2. Click **Photos**.

3. Click **Your Photos**.

4. Click to open a photo, then click **Edit**.

5. Click ▾next to the current privacy setting (Example: **Friends**):

6. Select the audience you want to share the photo with. Keep in mind:

   ○ You can only edit the privacy settings for individual photos in certain albums, including **Profile Pictures** and **Cover Photos**.

7. Click **Done Editing**.

How do I adjust Superframe settings on my Portal?

1. From **Home** on your Portal, tap **Settings**.

2. Tap **Superframe** .

From here, you can control and adjust:

- **Superframe Speed** - Adjust the frequency that Superframe rotates through pictures and videos.

23

- **Photos –** Manage the photos that will display on Superframe.

- **Birthdays -** Set whether you'd like to see Birthday reminders for your contacts in Superframe.

- **Tips -** Set whether you'd like to see Portal feature and functionality tips in Superframe.

- **Weather -** Set whether you'd like to see the weather forecast for your area in Superframe. Your weather forecast will be based on the city associated with your Portal.

- **Active Favorites -** Set if you'd like to see when your favorites are online in Superframe.

- **Hidden Photos -** See all of your hidden Superframe photos and videos.

How do I add or remove photos from Superframe on my Portal?

You can select which Facebook photos you'd like to add to Superframe. You can also remove or hide photos at any time.

To add or remove Facebook photos from Superframe:

1. From **Home** on your Portal, tap **Settings**.

2. Tap **Superframe** .

3. Tap **Photos**.

4. Tap ◖ next to any albums you'd like to add to or remove from Superframe.

To hide Facebook photos from Superframe:

1. When Superframe is displayed on your Portal, tap •••next to your name.

2. Tap **Hide This Photo**.

To unhide photos from Superframe:

1. From **Home** on your Portal, tap **Settings**.

2. Tap the **Superframe** tab.

3. Tap **Hidden Photos**. You may need to confirm your login to make changes.

4. Tap the photo you'd like to unhide.

5. Tap **Recover**.

6. Tap **Show**.

How do I delete a photo I uploaded to Facebook?

You can only delete photos that you've uploaded to Facebook. Keep in mind that once a photo is deleted, you won't be able to get it back.

To remove your photo from Facebook:

1. Go to the photo you'd like to delete.

2. Click the photo to open it.

3. Hover over the photo and click **Options** in the bottom right.

4. Select **Delete This Photo**, then click **Delete**.

How do I remove apps from the Portal home screen?

1. From **Home** on your Portal, press and hold on any app until a small **X** appears on the corner of your apps.

2. Tap the **X** on the corner of the app you'd like to remove.

3. Tap **Done** when you've finished editing your apps.

Note: Removing an app from your Portal home screen doesn't disconnect your credentials or subscriptions from the app you have removed. It also doesn't remove any of your data associated with the app.

How do I download new apps to my Portal?

After you set up your Portal, you'll have a selection of apps already installed and a selection of apps available for download. Some apps may require additional account login, registration, or payment. App availability differs based on the location where you use Portal.

To add new apps to your Portal:

1. From **Home** on your Portal, tap **Apps**.

2. Tap the app you'd like to download.

Note: Some apps may require additional account login, registration, or payment.

How do I connect my Spotify, Pandora or iHeartRadio accounts to Portal

You can connect and play music through several streaming services on your Portal, including Spotify, Pandora and iHeartRadio.

App availability differs based on the location where you use Portal.

Once you connect your music account to Portal, you can play or control music using the touchscreen or using voice commands like: "Hey Portal, play a song" or "Hey Portal, I want to listen to jazz."

Spotify

To use Spotify, select **Spotify** from **Home** on your Portal. A Spotify Premium account isn't required to use Spotify on Portal.

To connect your Spotify Premium account:

1. From **Home** on your Portal, tap **Spotify**.

2. Tap **Connect Spotify.**

3. Follow the on-screen instructions to connect your Spotify account.

Pandora

To connect a Pandora account, you can use a Pandora, Pandora Plus, or Pandora Premium account. Pandora is only currently available if you use Portal in the US.

To connect Pandora:

1. From **Home** on your Portal, tap **Pandora**.

2. Tap **Connect Pandora**.

3. Follow the on-screen instructions to connect your Pandora account.

iHeartRadio

To use iHeartRadio, select **iHeartRadio** from **Home** on your Portal. An iHeartRadio account isn't required to use iHeartRadio on Portal. iHeartRadio is only currently available if you're using Portal in the US.

How do I adjust the brightness of my Portal display?

1. Swipe up from the bottom of your Portal display to view the Quick Controls.

2. Use the slider to adjust your Portal's brightness.

How do I adjust the volume on Portal?

You can control volume directly by tapping the volume buttons on your Portal, or by swiping up from the bottom of your Portal screen to view the Quick Controls.

How do I use Portal safely with kids in my home?

- Set a 12-digit passcode to keep your screen locked when it's not in use.

- Turn your microphone and camera off when you aren't using your Portal, or use the included camera cover.

How do I add or remove Favorites from my Portal?

To add someone to your favorites using Portal:

1. From **Home** on your Portal, tap **Contacts**.

2. Tap the contact you want to add to your favorites.

3. Tap **Favorite**.

To remove someone from your favorites using Portal:

1. Under **Favorites,** tap the contact you'd like to remove.

2. Tap **Favorited.**

To add someone to your favorites from the Portal app:

1. Open the Portal app on your mobile device.

2. Tap the Portal you'd like to manage.

3. Tap **Favorites.**

4. Tap **Add a Favorite.**

5. Tap the name of any contact and then tap **Add.**

To remove someone from your favorites from the Portal app:

1. Open the Portal app on your mobile device.

2. Tap the Portal you'd like to manage.

3. Tap **Favorites.**

4. Tap the contact you'd like to remove from favorites.

5. Tap ◖ next to **Favorite.**

What information is collected for "Hey Portal"?

When Portal hears the wake word, "Hey Portal," it will start to record your voice interaction and create a computer-generated transcription of the recording. Like other voice assistants, when Portal is activated, it will also pick up other sounds in the immediate area beyond just the voice command - this may include ambient noise or nearby background conversations.

A voice command is something you ask Portal to do, such as "Hey Portal, call Mom" or "Hey Portal, what's the weather today?" Ambient noise or background conversation is any conversation or noise that happens in the background when you say a voice command that gets picked up by Portal. And a "false wake" recording is when Portal mistakenly hears the wake word and starts to record. When Portal is recording, you'll see a visual confirmation at the bottom of the screen. As Portal improves over time, it will get better at identifying and reducing the number of "false wakes," so you can have a better "Hey Portal" experience.

How does "Hey Portal" work with other voice services?

"Hey Portal" works independently from other voice services such as Amazon Alexa. If you activate Alexa on Portal and use the "Alexa" wake word, Amazon will process that request independently. Use of Alexa or any other third party voice services on Portal is subject to the terms and policies of those other services, not the terms and policies of Facebook and its products. Facebook doesn't collect voice interactions processed by a third party voice service.

How long do you keep my "Hey Portal" voice interactions?

Stored "Hey Portal" voice interactions are kept on Facebook servers for up to 3 years. We delete "false wakes" within 90 days of detection. When we delete voice interactions, they will no longer appear in your Portal Settings or Facebook Activity Log and will be deleted from our systems and no longer used as part of our human review or machine processes. You can always delete your "Hey Portal" voice interactions in Portal Settings or your Facebook Activity Log. Alternatively, you can turn off storage of your "Hey Portal" voice interactions in Portal Settings.

Can other people using my Portal see and access my voice interactions and settings?

Portal can be shared among multiple owners. If your Portal is shared, then all "Hey Portal" voice interactions and settings for that device will be accessible to you and the other owners. This means that other owners with whom you share your Portal will be able to see, hear and delete your voice interactions. Those people will also be able to turn off storage of "Hey Portal" voice interactions. If an owner is removed from your Portal, that person will no longer be able to perform these actions.

Do you share my 'Hey Portal' voice requests with anyone else?

Some third party apps or services on Portal, like Spotify, will respond to your "Hey Portal" voice commands. In order for this to work, Portal sends a text version of your "Hey Portal" voice command to the third party providing that app or service.

We also may share "Hey Portal" voice interactions with a third party if the law requires us to do so.

How do you use my 'Hey Portal' voice interactions?

"Hey Portal" voice interactions are used in a few different ways. Primarily, they are used to process and carry out your voice command. When you say "Hey Portal," your voice command is sent to Facebook's servers in real-time to process and respond to your request. We use stored "Hey Portal" voice interactions to help make our voice services get smarter, more accurate and better for everyone. We use a combination of human review and machine processes to troubleshoot and train our speech recognition systems. Lastly, we use "Hey Portal" voice commands to promote safety and integrity, and to help keep people safe on and off Facebook products.

How does "Hey Portal" work?

"Hey Portal" is a wake word that lets you use your Portal hands-free. If available to you, simply say "Hey Portal" when you want Portal to start a video call, check the weather or respond to other commands. Portal activates when it hears "Hey Portal" and gives you a visual confirmation at the bottom of the screen. When your Portal hears the wake word, it will start to record your voice interaction and send it to Facebook servers in real-time to respond to your request. When you turn Portal's microphone off, Portal won't listen for the wake word, and voice control will be disabled.

How do I control how Portal handles my voice interactions?

Portal offers clear and simple settings to control your voice interactions. You can choose to turn off storage of your "Hey Portal" voice interactions in Portal Settings. Even if you turn off storage, you can still use "Hey Portal" but the feature may not work as well. When storage is turned off, we won't keep recordings or transcripts of your voice interactions, which means you won't be able to view, hear or delete them. And we won't use those voice interactions to improve our voice services and they won't be reviewed by people. We'll still log system activity, such as the timestamp for when a voice interaction was made and the general category of the voice interaction. For example, if you said,

"Hey Portal, what's the weather in Seattle," we would simply categorize your question as "get weather." Any "Hey Portal" voice interactions made before you turned off storage will still be stored. You can easily view, hear and delete your "Hey Portal" voice interactions and transcriptions in Portal Settings or your Facebook Activity Log.

How do I use voice interactions with my Portal?

"Hey Portal" and Alexa are built into your Portal for hands-free control. In order to enable Alexa on your Portal, one of the accounts linked to your device must sign in to their Amazon account.

You can use "Hey Portal" to control things like:

- Calling.
- Weather.
- Time.

- Brightness control.

- Video control.

- Using camera Effects.

You can use Alexa to control things like:

- Playing music through music services connected to your Amazon account.

- Settings alarms or timers.

- Shopping and creating to-do lists.

- Some Alexa-supported features, like controlling smart-home devices.

For example:

- Set an alarm by saying, "Alexa, set an alarm."

- Start a video call by saying, "Hey Portal, call [contact name]" or "Hey Portal, call [Relationship Name]."

- Hear the local weather, birthdays, events and news by saying, "Hey Portal, good morning."

- The Alexa account connected to Portal isn't linked to a particular Portal account. If one of multiple Portal accounts is removed from your Portal, the Alexa app will remain connected on the device.

- You can also disconnect Alexa by using the Alexa app.

How do I enable Alexa on my Portal?

To use Alexa on your Portal, you must connect an Amazon Alexa account to your Portal. You can connect to Alexa during the Settings .

To connect Alexa:

1. From **Home** , tap **Settings**.
2. Tap **Accounts.**

3. Tap **Amazon Alexa** and follow the on-screen instructions to log in with your Amazon account or to disconnect Alexa.

To deregister Alexa:

1. From Home, tap **Settings.**

2. Tap **Accounts.**

3. Tap **Amazon Alexa.**

4. Tap **Device Options.**

5. Tap **Deregister.**

6. Tap **OK.**

Notes:

- The Alexa account connected to Portal isn't linked to a particular Portal account. If one of multiple Portal accounts is removed from your Portal, the Alexa app will remain connected on the device.

'Hey Portal' and Alexa don't understand me.

If "Hey Portal" and Alexa have trouble understanding you:

- Make sure your Portal's microphone is turned on.

- Make sure your camera cover is not covering your Portal's microphone.

- Speak towards your Portal and move closer if necessary.

- Check to see if "Hey Portal" is available to you.

How To connect your WhatsApp account to your Portal:

1. From **Home,** tap **Settings.**

2. Tap **Accounts.**

3. Tap **[Your name].**

4. Tap **Connect WhatsApp.** You may be asked to confirm your login to make changes.

5. Tap the box next to **By checking, you agree to receive messages on WhatsApp,** then tap **Continue.**

6. Tap **Continue** and follow the on-screen instructions.

7. Tap **Done.**

Note: Some features, including "Hey Portal," are not available when you log in with WhatsApp or when a WhatsApp login exists on a shared device.

How do I view regulatory information about my Portal?

To view your Portal's regulatory information:

1. From **Home** on your Portal, tap **Settings.**

2. Tap the **About** tab and then tap **Regulatory.**

How do I put my Portal in "sleep" mode?

You can put your Portal in "sleep" mode, which turns the screen off, but allows your Portal to be woken up by touch, voice commands, motion detection or incoming calls. Your Portal will go to sleep automatically after 15 minutes without use, or you can make your Portal sleep manually.

To make your Portal sleep:

1. Swipe up from the bottom of your Portal screen to view the Quick Controls.

2. Tap ⏻.

What comes with my Portal?

Before you set up your Portal, make sure you have all the items that should be included in your Portal box.

The following items should be included in your Portal or Portal Mini box:

- Portal or Portal Mini.

- Power cord.

- Quick Start Guide.

How do I set up or change the Wi-Fi network on my Portal?

During the initial setup of your Portal, you'll choose and connect to a Wi-Fi network. You can change your Portal's Wi-Fi network at any time.

To change your Portal's Wi-Fi network:

1. From **Home** on your Portal, tap **Settings**.

2. Tap **Wi-Fi**.

3. Select the network you'd like to connect to, enter your Wi-Fi password, and tap **Join**.

If your Portal can't find or connect to your Wi-Fi network, try the following:

- Make sure your Wi-Fi router is on and connected to the internet.

- Make sure your Portal is in range of your Wi-Fi router. Move your Portal closer to your Wi-Fi router if necessary.

- Unplug your Portal, modem and router, plug them back in and try again.

To enter your Wi-Fi network manually:

1. From **Home** , tap **Settings**.

2. Tap Wi-Fi.

3. Tap **Other Network** and enter your Wi-Fi network name.

4. Select your Wi-Fi network's security method from the dropdown, enter your Wi-Fi password and tap **Join**.

I'm having trouble using the touch screen while setting up my Portal.

If your Portal's touch screen isn't working as expected during setup, accessibility options may have been turned on by mistake. If you're seeing a green rectangle on your

Portal's screen or Portal is reading text out loud to you during setup, accessibility options have been turned on.

To turn accessibility options off during setup:

1. Use two or more fingers to press and hold your Portal's touch screen for 8 seconds. After 4 seconds, you'll hear an audible prompt to continue holding your Portal screen to turn accessibility options off.

2. Continue holding for 8 seconds to turn off accessibility options.

To use your Portal with accessibility options turned on:

- Scroll by using two fingers.

- Select by double-tapping the screen where you'd like to make a selection.

How do I take care of my Portal?

To take care of your Portal, follow these tips:

Picking a location

- Set up your Portal on a flat, stable surface where it's not likely to tip or fall.

- Set up and keep your Portal indoors in a well-ventilated, climate-controlled location. Your Portal may get warm during use, which is normal.

- Keep your Portal and its cord away from food, water or other liquids.

- Keep your Portal and its cord away from sources of heat like stoves, ovens or radiators.

Cord care

- When setting up Portal, plug the cord into the device first, then into an appropriate outlet.

- Arrange the cord so it's out of reach for children and pets, and no one will trip on it.

- Shut down and unplug your Portal before moving it.

- Unplug your Portal's cord from the outlet first, then from the device.

- Only use the included power cord with your Portal.

Cleaning your Portal:

- Use a clean, soft dry cloth to clean the screen and outside of your Portal.

- Only clean the outside of your Portal. Don't attempt to open your Portal or to clean inside any ventilation or other openings.

- Don't use compressed air to clean your Portal.

- Don't use abrasive or harsh chemicals when cleaning your Portal.

How do I know if my contacts are available to call on my Portal?

Contacts who have a •next to their name are recently active on their Portal, Messenger or Facebook. If someone has set to allow you to see when they're home on Portal, you'll see a when they're home and available to call.

How do I call my Portal using the Portal app?

To call your Portal from the Portal app:

1. Open the Portal app.

2. Tap the Portal device you want to call.

3. Tap **Call Portal.**

Note: The Portal app doesn't currently support calling or photo sharing to Portals that have been set up with WhatsApp only.

How do I hide a suggested or recent contact?

You can hide suggested or recent contacts from **Home.**

To hide a suggested or recent contact:

1. From **Home**, press and hold the contact you want to hide.

2. Tap ×.

3. Tap 🏠.

How do I control the camera during a call on Portal?

During a call you can move around the room and talk freely while Portal's Smart Camera and Smart Sound adjust to keep you audible and in the frame. You can also manually adjust the zoom and focus of your camera using gestures on your Portal's touchscreen.

To enter Manual Mode you can:

- In self view, use a pinch gesture to zoom in or out.

- In self view, use a drag gesture to change the area of focus.

To turn off Manual Mode:

- On the bottom right corner of your Portal screen, tap 🔲.

To have your camera focus on one individual (Spotlight) during a call:

- Tap the persons face in yourself view.

- When you see a yellow frame around their face, tap their face again.

To turn off Spotlight during a call:

- In self view, double-tap the face of the person who is in Spotlight.

Note: If the person you're calling is also on a Portal device, you can adjust the focus of each other's cameras by using the same gestures in yourself view.

How do I change the Call Settings on my Portal?

Call Settings allow you to set when you receive incoming calls on Portal. You can select Do Not Disturb, which silences your calls and shows you as not active until 8AM. Call Settings can be uniquely set for each account on your Portal.

To change your Call Settings:

1. From **Home** on your Portal, tap **Settings.**

2. Under **Call Settings,** tap ◖next to **Do Not Disturb.**

Who can I call or receive calls from on Portal?

Making calls on Portal:

On Portal you can call the Facebook friends, Messenger connections and WhatsApp contacts of any accounts linked to your Portal. you can use your Portal to call friends located in any country where the Messenger app or WhatsApp are supported.

Receiving calls on Portal:

Currently, Portal calls can only be received from other Portal devices, from WhatsApp on mobile devices, from the Messenger app on mobile devices or tablets, from messenger.com or from facebook.com. Portal can't be called from Messenger Kids accounts or the Messenger Lite app.

Your Portal contacts:

Your Portal contacts are the Facebook friends, Messenger connections and WhatsApp contacts of all accounts linked to your Portal. If you share a Portal with others, all accounts that have been linked to your Portal will share contacts on Portal. Anyone who shares your Portal will have access to the contacts on the device and will be able to make and answer calls.

Viewing your Portal contacts:

From **Home** on your Portal, tap **Contacts.** From there, you can browse by **Suggested** contacts, **Recent** contacts or contacts by account type.

How can my contacts see when I'm available on Portal?

You can control how your contacts see whether or not you are active and available on Portal through the **Facebook Active Status** setting.

The **Facebook Active Status** setting allows your contacts to see when your Portal is active or recently active. You'll appear active or recently active unless you turn off the setting every place you're using Messenger or Facebook. This setting also affects whether you can see when your friends and contacts are active or recently active.

To change your Facebook Active Status on Portal:

1. From **Home** on your Portal, tap **Settings.**

2. Tap **Privacy.**

3. Under **Permissions,** tap **Facebook Active Status.**

4. Tap ◌to turn your **Facebook Active Status** on or off.

How do I make group calls on my Portal?

Group calls with Messenger connections:

With Portal, you can add up to 7 Messenger connections to a call for a total of 8 people, including yourself. You or other connections on your call can add any Facebook friends or Messenger connections to your call. You can't have both Messenger and WhatsApp users on the same call.

Group calls with WhatsApp contacts:

With Portal, you can add up to 3 WhatsApp contacts to a call for a total of 4 people, including yourself. You or other contacts on your call can add any WhatsApp contacts to your call. In order to call any WhatsApp contact from your Portal, the contact must have WhatsApp open or in standby mode on their mobile phone.

You can't have both Messenger and WhatsApp users on the same call.

To make a group call on your Portal:

1. Start a call with one of the contacts you'd like to join the group call.

2. During the call, tap the screen to view the menu.

3. Tap and then tap the person or people you'd like to add to your call.

How do I connect Bluetooth devices to my Portal?

Using Bluetooth, you can pair headphones to your Portal or use Portal as a speaker. Before connecting a Bluetooth device to your Portal, make sure your device has Bluetooth turned on and is in pairing or discoverability mode.

To connect a Bluetooth device to your Portal:

1. From **Home** on your Portal, tap **Settings**.

2. Tap **Bluetooth.**

3. Tap the toggle next to **Bluetooth** to turn Bluetooth discoverability on.

4. Tap **Pair Device**.

5. Select your Bluetooth device from the **Available Devices** list on your Portal or

select your Portal from the Bluetooth settings on your device to pair the device.

How do I change the weather location I see on Superframe?

Your Portal will set your city automatically and will show you local weather information on Superframe based on that location. You can also set your city setting manually.

To set your city manually:

1. From **Home** on your Portal, tap **Settings**.

2. Tap **City.**

3. Tap the toggle next to **Set City Manually.**

4. Tap **City** and enter the ZIP code you'd like to set.

5. Select your city.

How do I update the software on my Portal?

Your Portal software will update automatically when connected to Wi-Fi and turned on. In order to make sure your Portal software updates automatically:

- Ensure your Portal is turned on and connected to Wi-Fi when leaving your Portal idle.

- Allow your Portal to remain idle for up to 3 hours to ensure it updates to the latest software version.

How do I adjust the accessibility settings on my Portal?

1. From **Home** on your Portal, tap **Settings.**

2. Tap **Accessibility** .

From here you can control and adjust:

- Font Size

- High Contrast Text

- Color Inversion

- Color Correction

- Triple-tap for Magnification

- Touch and Hold Delay

- Vision Accessibility Options

- Captions

Notes:

- Portal doesn't currently support closed captions during video calls.

Portal doesn't ring when I call from the Messenger app.

If a Portal doesn't ring after an attempted call, you may be on a version Messenger that is incompatible with Portal. Your Messenger app should automatically update to the compatible version within 30 to 60 minutes of your attempted call.

To make sure you're on a compatible version of the Messenger app:

1. Download the latest version of Messenger on your phone or tablet.

2. Attempt a call to a Portal device from the Messenger app.

   o If the attempted call does not ring on Portal, wait 60 minutes and try again.

Notes:

- Additional interactions with Portal and the Messenger app, like being added to a Portal's Favorites list or receiving a call from Portal, will automatically update you to the compatible Messenger app after 30 to 60 minutes.

How do I install or update the Messenger app?

When you install the latest version of the Messenger app, you get the newest features. Updating the Messenger app may also help to fix problems when something's not working.

To install or update the Messenger app:

Android

- Messenger for Android from the Google Play Store

iPhone or iPad

- Messenger for iPhone or iPad from the App Store

Windows

Download link.

To check for updates:

1. Open the Messenger App for Windows.

2. Click ≡ in the top left.

3. Hover over **Messenger**, and then select **Check for Updates**.

How do I perform a factory reset on my Portal?

Resetting your Portal will set the device to its original factory settings and will disconnect any accounts, erase any preferences, local device data and or settings you've set on the device.

To perform a factory reset on your Portal using the touch screen:

1. From **Home** on your Portal, tap **Settings**.

2. Scroll down and tap **Factory Reset**. If prompted, select who's making changes to your Portal settings and log in with your Facebook account?

3. Tap **Reset** to complete a factory reset on your Portal.

To manually perform a factory reset on your Portal or Portal Mini:

1. Unplug your Portal.

2. Press and hold both the Volume Down and Volume Up buttons and plug your Portal back in at the same time.

You will get an on-screen notification that your Portal will factory reset in 10 seconds.

My Portal's display is going black or flickering.

If your Portal's display is going black or flickering, try unplugging your Portal and plugging it back in again.

My Portal's display is pixelated, blurry, or freezing during calls.

If your calls are pixelated, blurry or freezing during a call, you or the person you're calling may have a weak signal and you should try the following:

- Check your Wi-Fi signal. If your signal is weak, move your Portal closer to your Wi-Fi router or reset the device.

- Make sure the person you're calling with has a strong signal on their Portal or phone.

It's hard for me to hear others during calls on my Portal.

If you're experiencing issues hearing others during calls on Portal, try:

- Adjusting the volume.

- Checking your Wi-Fi signal strength.

- Unplugging your Portal, plugging it back in and trying the call again.

How do I check my Wi-Fi signal?

To check the strength of your internet connection:

1. From **Home** on your Portal, tap **Settings**.

2. Under **Device Settings**, tap **Wi-Fi**.

3. Next to your Wi-Fi network, tap the **I** button.

How can I share feedback with my experience with Portal?

If you'd like to submit feature or functionality requests, you can use our Portal User voice channel. The Portal User voice channel allows other Portal users to up vote submitted ideas for our team to review.

If you've discovered broken features or bugs while on Portal, you can use the feedback tool from the **Help** section of your Portal **Settings** menu to submit them to our team.

To use the on-device feedback tool:

1. From **Home** on your Portal, tap **Settings**.

2. Tap **Help**.

3. Tap **Give Feedback on Portal**.

4. Tap the category that applies to your feedback, then use the on-screen keyboard to type your feedback.

5. Tap **Send** to submit your feedback.

How do I use Workplace on Portal?

To start using Workplace on Portal:

1. From **Home,** tap to open the **Workplace** app.

2. Tap **Connect Workplace.** Go to workplace.com/device in a different browser and enter the on-screen code.

3. On your Portal, tap **Get Started.**

4. Set a 4-digit PIN. You will need to enter your PIN before you answer calls.

Can I go live on Facebook using my Portal?

To use Facebook Live on Portal Mini

From **Home**, tap to open the **Facebook Live** app. You can choose your audience and **Add a description.**

1. Tap **Start Live Video.**

When you go live on Facebook, your live broadcast will share in stories and as a post.

During a live broadcast on Portal, you can view things like:

- How many people are watching

- Comments

- Reactions

How do I use the Browser on my Portal?

With the Browser app on Portal, you can access websites with regular or incognito browsing, save bookmarks, adjust browser settings, and pin select websites to your Portal's **Home** for direct access.

Browsing

To browse websites on Portal:

1. From **Home** on your Portal, tap **Browser**.

2. Tap the **Address Bar**.

3. Use the on-screen keyboard to search or enter a website address.

To browse in incognito mode:

1. From **Home** on your Portal, tap **Browser**.

2. At the top right of your browser window, tap ⋮ and then tap **New incognito tab**.

To view the desktop version of a website:

1. From **Home** on your Portal, tap **Browser**.

2. Navigate to a website.

3. At the top right of your browser window, tap ⋮ and then tap **Desktop site**.

Settings and Tips

To add a website to Home on your Portal:

1. From **Home** on your Portal, tap **Portal Apps**.

2. At the top of the screen, tap the **Websites** tab.

3. Tap the website you'd like to pin to your Portal's **Home**.

To go back or return to Home from a full-screen video:

1. While in full-screen, use a dragging gesture from the top of your Portal screen downward.

2. Tap the **Back** or **Home** button from the drop-down menu.

To change your Browser settings:

1. From **Home** on your Portal, tap **Browser**.

2. At the top right of your browser window, tap ⋮ and then tap **Settings**.

From Settings you can control the following in-browser settings:

- Your default search engine.

- Password settings.

- Notification settings.

- Your startup page.

- Privacy settings.

- Accessibility settings.

- Site settings.

- Language settings.

How do I set up a pass code for my Portal?

You can set a 4-12 digit pass code to keep your screen locked when it's not in use. The pass code will be required to return to Home from Superframe, but you can still use voice commands to make and receive calls.

While your Portal is locked, you won't be able to add additional contacts to a call.

To set your Portal pass code:

1. From **Home** on your Portal, Tap **Settings.**

2. Tap the **Privacy** tab and then tap **Pass code.**

3. Enter the 4-12 digit passcode for your device and tap the **Checkmark**.

4. Re-enter your 4-12 digit passcode and tap the **Checkmark** to confirm your passcode.

To change your Portal passcode:

1. From **Home** on your Portal, Tap **Settings.**

2. Tap the **Privacy** tab and then tap **Change Passcode**.

3. Select who's making changes and log in with your Facebook account.

4. Enter your old passcode and tap the **Checkmark**.

5. Enter your new passcode, reenter the new passcode, and then tap the **Checkmark** to confirm your new passcode.

How do I share music while on a call?

During a call with other Portal users, you can share music using Spotify, Pandora or iHeartRadio with friends who also have accounts linked to their Portals. App availability differs based on the location where you use Portal.

By sharing music during a call, you and your friends can listen to the same songs at the same time.

To share music during a call:

1. During a call, tap the screen to view the call menu.

2. Tap and then tap **Spotify, Pandora** or **iHeartRadio**.

3. Select the song or station you'd like to share.

4. On the receiving Portal, select **Accept.**

You can also share music from the Spotify or Pandora mobile apps by selecting your Portal as your output device during a call. The person on the receiving end of music sharing can take over playback control by following the instructions above and sharing a song from their Portal.

Why do I have to log in with Facebook to view or edit certain settings on my Portal?

Some settings require you to confirm your Facebook login to make sure you are the one viewing or editing these settings on your Portal.

You can control this with the following options:

- If you have already confirmed your login status in **Settings** on your Portal and don't close the **Settings** menu, you won't be required to re-authenticate your status to access some settings for a short period of time.

- During your initial Portal setup or when accessing some settings on your Portal, selecting the checkbox next to **Don't ask me to confirm my login again** will allow you to access some settings without logging in again with Facebook.

Notes:

- Some settings will always require authentication, such as when new accounts are added to Portal.

- If you allow access to some settings without logging in again with Facebook, anyone who has access to your Portal will be able to view and edit those settings.

Why am I being asked to log in to my Portal again?

Reasons you may be asked to log in again include:

- You changed your Facebook password.

- Multiple accounts are logged in on your Portal and one of the accounts got logged out.

- Multiple accounts are logged in on your Portal and one of the accounts changed their Facebook password.

- There was a software update on your Portal.

To log back in to your Portal, follow the on-screen instructions.

Does Portal have parental controls?

- Portal does not support Messenger Kids and calls cannot be made to or from Messenger Kids accounts on Portal.

- You must have an active Facebook account and therefore be 13 years of age or older to log into Portal.

Thank you for purchasing our guide!

Printed in Great Britain
by Amazon